FOREWORD

THIS BOOK is about the fascinating world in which we live, and the mysterious void called space through which our planet Earth travels, along with countless millions of other heavenly bodies.

For thousands of years, mankind has gazed at the night sky and tried to unlock its secrets. Today, thanks to the knowledge gained by astronomers and other scientists over the centuries, together with advances in modern technology, we are beginning to gain a fuller understanding of the structure of space and even its origins.

Likewise, information about our planet has been built up steadily through the work of geologists and the many other scientists who study the Earth.

This book answers many of the questions about Earth and space frequently asked by young readers. The popular question and answer format provides clear, concise answers, all of which are accompanied by superb, full-colour illustrations.

Beginning with the mysteries of the Universe, the structure of stars and planets and the exploration of space, the book then describes the structure of the Earth and the forces that shape it. Finally, the reader can then find answers to many questions about the evolution of life, the world's countries and the lives of people today.

It is hoped that this book will encourage readers to seek more information about the universe and our world within it.

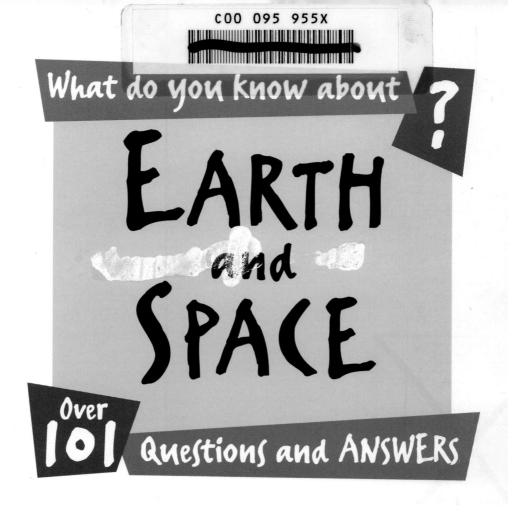

What do you know about ?

EARTH and SPACE

Over 101 Questions and ANSWERS

Written by Ian Graham,
Andrew Langley & Paul Sterry

Vineyard
BOOKS

Photo Credits
p.6 Royal Observatory, Edinburgh; p.7 Science Photo Library/Mt Palomar
Observatory; p.13 NASA; p.21 Jerome Yeats/Science Photo Library.

Planned and produced by
Andromeda Oxford Limited
11-15 The Vineyard
Abingdon
Oxon OX14 3PX

ISBN 1 86199 028 6

Printed in Singapore

CONTENTS

MYSTERIOUS UNIVERSE

Q **How did the Sun and planets form?**

A Nobody knows for certain. Most scientists think that the Sun, Earth and other planets (the Solar System) were formed from a mass of dust and gas. Nearly 5,000 million years ago, this mass started to shrink, and then spin and flatten into a disc. The centre of the disc spun fastest. This became the Sun. The rest of the material turned into the planets (below).

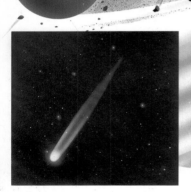

Q **What is a meteor?**

A A meteor is a sudden streak of light in the sky (above). It is caused by a piece of rock from outer space entering the Earth's atmosphere. The friction causes it to burn up.

Q **What is a nebula?**

A A nebula is a cloud of dust and gas in space. Some of the clouds block out the light from the stars behind. These are called dark nebulae. One of the best-known is the Horsehead Nebula (right). Other dust clouds reflect the light from the stars and shine brightly. These are called bright nebulae.

A Sometimes – no-one knows why – stars collapse in on themselves. This increases their gravity (a force that pulls everything inwards). Nothing escapes – not even light. These very dense bodies are called black holes (below).

Q What is a galaxy?

A A galaxy (below) is a huge spinning mass of stars in outer space. There are millions of galaxies, each containing billions of stars as well as gas and dust. Our galaxy is called the Milky Way. It contains about 200,000 million stars.

Q How did the Universe begin?

A Many scientists believe that all the material of the Universe was once crammed together in one place. Then, about 15,000 million years ago, an explosion or 'Big Bang' occurred. The material of the Universe flew out in all directions, forming galaxies and other bodies, mainly gas and dust. The effects of this explosion are still continuing, causing the Universe to expand (right). The galaxies still seem to be rushing away from each other.

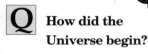

Galaxies

SOLAR SYSTEM

Altitude
in km

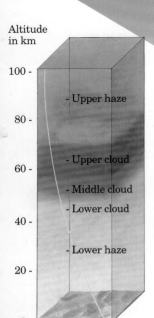

100 -

- Upper haze

80 -

- Upper cloud

60 -

- Middle cloud

- Lower cloud

40 -

- Lower haze

20 -

0 -

Dish aerial

UHF Aerial

Cameras

Digging arm

Footpad

Q **Which is the hottest planet?**

A Venus. It is the second planet from the Sun. Venus is completely covered in dense clouds (left). These act like a giant greenhouse, raising temperatures to 462 °C. Several probes have landed on Venus but none has survived.

Q **Is there life on Mars?**

A In 1976 two Viking probes (above) landed on Mars and sent pictures of the rocky surface back to Earth. There were no astronauts aboard the Viking probes, so automatic soil samplers tested the red, dry soil for any sign of life. None was found.

Q **Which planets have rings?**

A Jupiter, Saturn, Uranus and Neptune have rings. The rings are actually tiny pieces of rock covered with ice. Rings may be fragments of moons which were destroyed, or they may have been part of the planets.

Q **How large is our Sun?**

A The Sun (below) has a diameter of 1,320,000 kilometres. Its volume is approximately 1.3 million times larger than the Earth's. However, the Sun is only a medium-sized star; many stars are much bigger. By comparison, the biggest planet in our Solar System is Jupiter (143,000 km diameter), and the smallest is Pluto (2,000 km diameter).

Jupiter

Mercury

Venus

Earth

Mars

Sun

Q How hot is the Sun?

A The Sun is a vast ball of glowing gas (right). At the
heart of the Sun, temperatures are thought to be
15,000,000 °C! The heat is created in the core, or centre,
by the nuclear fusion of hydrogen atoms. This is similar to
the process that occurs in an exploding hydrogen bomb.
Marks on the Sun, called sunspots, appear dark only
because they are 1,200 °C cooler than the surrounding gas.
Solar flares are great tongues of gas. All life on Earth is
dependent upon the light and heat from the Sun.

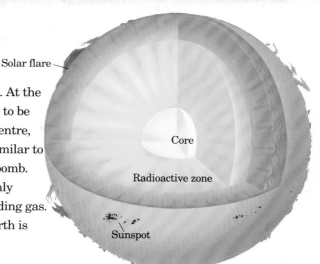

Solar flare

Core

Radioactive zone

Sunspot

Q How do we know so much about the
planets?

A Space probes travel through the Solar
System sending information back to Earth.
Space probes carry cameras to take pictures, as
well as equipment to detect the presence of radio
waves and magnetic fields.

TV Camera

Dish aerial

Thruster

Electronics
compartment

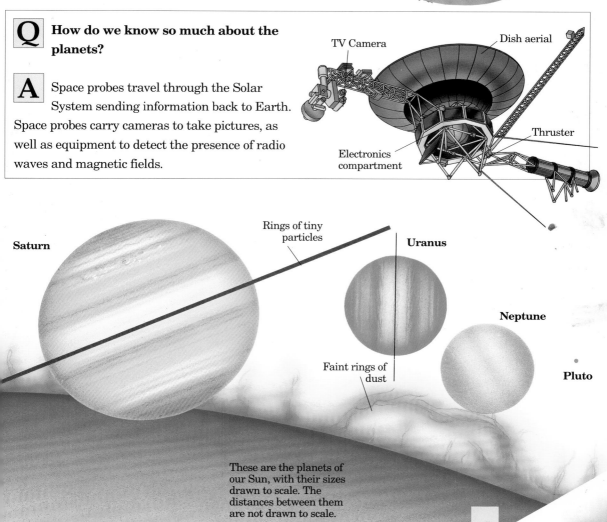

Saturn

Rings of tiny
particles

Uranus

Neptune

Pluto

Faint rings of
dust

These are the planets of
our Sun, with their sizes
drawn to scale. The
distances between them
are not drawn to scale.

THE PLANETS

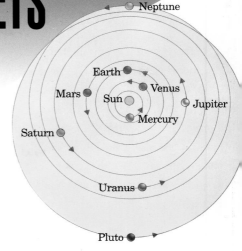

Q What are planets made of?

A The planets that are closest to the Sun, from Mercury to Mars, are small, rocky worlds. They have a metal centre, or core, surrounded by a thick mantle of rock with a thin, rocky crust on the surface. The outer planets are very different. Jupiter and Saturn are made mostly of hydrogen. Uranus and Neptune have a rocky core surrounded by ice and hydrogen (below). Pluto is made of rock, with an icy coating.

Core

Hydrogen

Saturn

Core

Hydrogen and ice

Uranus

Q How do the planets orbit the Sun?

A All the planets in the Solar System travel in the same direction around the Sun (above). Their paths are slightly flattened circles called ellipses. Pluto's orbit is pushed so much to one side that it crosses Neptune's orbit

Q What are planets?

A Planets are worlds that orbit the Sun. The word 'planet' comes from a Greek word meaning wanderer, because of the strange wandering paths they appear to have when seen from Earth. There are nine planets (right). Mercury is the closest to the Sun, then Venus, Earth, Mars, Jupiter, Saturn, Uranus, Neptune and Pluto.

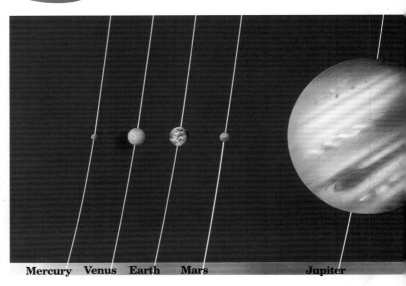

Mercury Venus Earth Mars Jupiter

Q What is the Great Red Spot?

A Jupiter's Great Red Spot (below) is a swirling storm 30,000 kilometres across. It was first seen by astronomers as long ago as 1664. Storms on Earth last a few weeks at most. The Great Red Spot has lasted for centuries because Jupiter has no solid surface to slow it down.

Great Red Spot

Q Which planets have moons?

A Only Mercury and Venus do not have moons. Earth has one moon. Mars has two (above). Jupiter has 16 moons. One of them, Ganymede, is larger than the planet Mercury. Saturn has 19 moons, Uranus 15, Neptune eight while Pluto has only one.

Q What are the canals of Mars?

A Over the centuries, astronomers thought that the dark lines and patches on the surface of Mars might be canals, built by an ancient civilization for carrying water. However, none of these so-called canals are visible in photographs taken by probes sent from Earth to Mars. Therefore scientists now believe that the canals are probably an optical illusion.

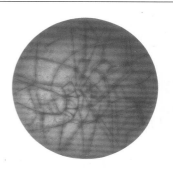

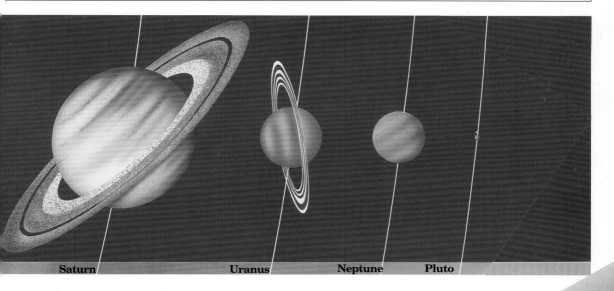

Saturn   **Uranus**   **Neptune**   **Pluto**

MOON

Q Why does the Moon seem to change shape?

A The Moon shines because it reflects light from the Sun. However, as it travels around the Earth, we see more or less of its surface, making it appear to change in shape. The different shapes are called phases (below).

Q What is inside the Moon?

A No-one has ever examined the inside of the Moon (below). Its outside looks very different from the Earth, but inside it is probably the same. Beneath the thin outer crust is a mantle of solid rock. Under this is a thinner layer of molten rock, and at the centre is the core, about 1,420 kilometres from the surface.

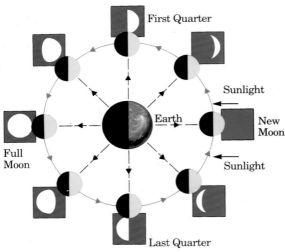

First Quarter

Sunlight

New Moon

Earth

Full Moon

Sunlight

Last Quarter

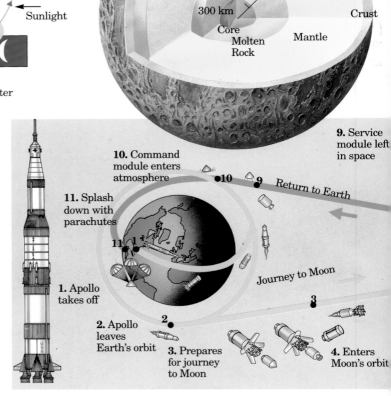

70 km

1,000 km

350 km

300 km

Core
Molten
Rock

Mantle

Crust

Q When did people first land on the Moon?

A The Apollo 11 spacecraft (right) took off in July 1969. It was carried by a huge Saturn rocket for the first stage of its journey. Shooting out of Earth's orbit, Apollo travelled to the Moon. The lunar module separated and landed on the Moon's surface. Two of the crew, Neil Armstrong and Edwin Aldrin, became the first people to walk on the Moon.

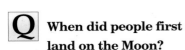

9. Service module left in space

10. Command module enters atmosphere

11. Splash down with parachutes

Return to Earth

Journey to Moon

1. Apollo takes off

2. Apollo leaves Earth's orbit

3. Prepares for journey to Moon

4. Enters Moon's orbit

Q What is on the surface of the Moon?

A The Moon's surface (right) is covered with dust and rocks which have been smashed to pieces by showers of rock-like objects called meteorites. It is pitted with craters, also caused by meteorites. Most are just tiny dents, but some are hundreds of kilometres wide. Some areas of the Moon look dark. People once thought these areas were seas. They were formed when meteorites cracked the Moon's surface. Molten rock bubbled up from below and grew hard. There are also many high mountains and deep valleys.

Fuel tank

Service module

Main engine nozzle

Thruster

Command module

Lunar module

Ladder

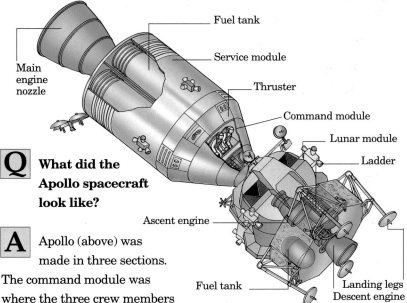

Ascent engine

Fuel tank

Landing legs
Descent engine

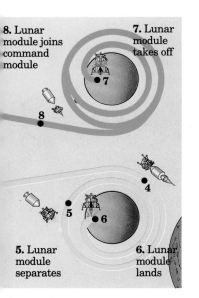

8. Lunar module joins command module

7. Lunar module takes off

● 7

8 ●

● 4

5 ● 6

5. Lunar module separates

6. Lunar module lands

Q What did the Apollo spacecraft look like?

A Apollo (above) was made in three sections. The command module was where the three crew members lived for most of the journey. Behind this was the service module. This contained the rocket engine and tanks for fuel and oxygen. The lunar module was used for landing on the Moon. It had four legs which spread out to support it on the Moon's surface. The lunar module and service module were left behind in space. Only the command module returned to splash down in the Pacific Ocean.

EXPLORING THE HEAVENS

Q **How did early astronomers study the heavens?**

A Astronomers studied the sky with the naked eye until the 17th century. In 1609 the Italian astronomer Galileo Galilei (above) became the first person to study the sky with a telescope.

Q **What did Giotto tell us about comets?**

A In 1986, the Giotto space probe (below) studied Halley's Comet. A comet consists of a lump of rock and ice called the nucleus, inside a cloud of gas and dust called the coma (inset). It also has a bright tail. Giotto's photographs show a nucleus measuring 8 kilometres by 12 kilometres. Its instruments found that the coma and tail are made of dust and water vapour.

Q **How does a modern telescope work?**

A There are two types of telescope. A refractor uses a lens to form an image. A reflector uses a curved mirror. Most modern telescopes used in astronomy are reflectors. The telescope is finely balanced and turns slowly to keep the image steady as the Earth moves. A Schmidt telescope (right) is used to photograph large areas of the sky.

Schmidt telescope gathering light from the stars

Counterbalance

Inside the telescope

Mirror

Light rays

Eyepiece

Q Why is the Hubble Telescope in space?

A Light from distant stars passes through the Earth's atmosphere before it reaches a telescope on the ground. The swirling atmosphere makes the stars twinkle. Modern telescopes are usually built on top of mountains, where the atmosphere is thinner, to reduce this effect. The Hubble Space Telescope (below) can see more clearly than any telescope on Earth because it is above the atmosphere.

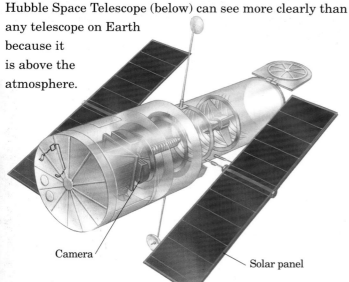

Camera

Solar panel

Q How did the Pioneer space probes work?

A Pioneer 10 and 11 (right) were the first spacecraft to visit the outer Solar System. They were designed to find out if a spacecraft could travel through the asteroid belt, a swarm of rocks orbiting the Sun between Mars and Jupiter. Most spacecraft use solar cells to make electricity from sunlight. Pioneer 10 and 11 travelled so far from the Sun that solar cells would not work. Instead, they carried nuclear power generators to make electricity.

Q Where did the Voyager space probes go?

A Voyager 1 and 2 were launched in 1977. The pull of gravity from the outer planets guided the spacecraft from one planet to the next. Voyager 1 flew past Jupiter in 1979 (below) and Saturn in 1980. Voyager 2 flew past Jupiter (1979), Saturn (1981), Uranus (1986) and Neptune (1989). Their cameras and instruments studied each planet. All the information was sent back to Earth by radio.

Pioneer 11

Thruster

Cosmic ray telescope

Nuclear power generator

SPACE TRAVEL

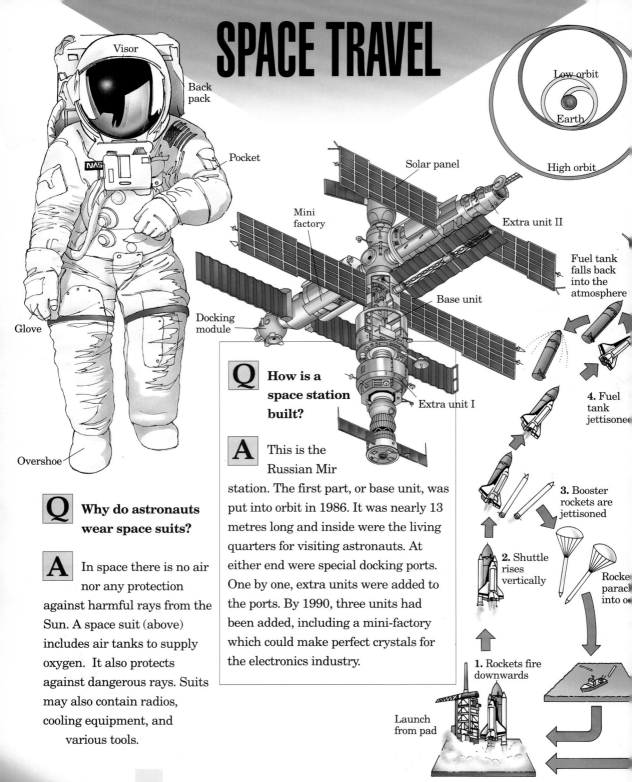

Visor

Back pack

Pocket

Glove

Overshoe

Low orbit

Earth

High orbit

Solar panel

Mini factory

Extra unit II

Fuel tank falls back into the atmosphere

Base unit

Docking module

Extra unit I

4. Fuel tank jettisoned

3. Booster rockets are jettisoned

Rocket parac into o

2. Shuttle rises vertically

1. Rockets fire downwards

Launch from pad

Q How is a space station built?

A This is the Russian Mir station. The first part, or base unit, was put into orbit in 1986. It was nearly 13 metres long and inside were the living quarters for visiting astronauts. At either end were special docking ports. One by one, extra units were added to the ports. By 1990, three units had been added, including a mini-factory which could make perfect crystals for the electronics industry.

Q Why do astronauts wear space suits?

A In space there is no air nor any protection against harmful rays from the Sun. A space suit (above) includes air tanks to supply oxygen. It also protects against dangerous rays. Suits may also contain radios, cooling equipment, and various tools.

Q What is an orbit?

A An orbit is the path an object takes around a star, planet or moon. Satellites circle the Earth in several different orbits (left). Those which take photographs use low orbits. High orbits are used by satellites which transmit signals such as television broadcasts.

5. Shuttle prepares for re-entry

Q How is the shuttle different from most spacecraft?

6. Shuttle glows red-hot as it enters atmosphere

A Most spacecraft fly only once and their rockets burn up in flight. The space shuttle (below) is unusual because the craft and booster rockets can be used again. This means scientists can spend money on equipment which would have been too expensive to use only once. Satellites and other equipment are stored in the payload bay for use in orbit. Orbiting satellites can be put into the payload bay and brought back to Earth for repair.

7. Shuttle tilts nose-down to glide

Fuel tank

Robot arm

Payload bay

8. Pilot steers shuttle towards landing ground

Q How do spacecraft get into space?

A To enter space, rockets must escape Earth's gravity. This requires a speed of 28,000 km/h. Such speeds are easiest to reach by vertical take-off. But it takes huge amounts of power to lift a spacecraft. The space shuttle has a big fuel tank and two booster rockets to supply this power.

Main thrust engine

Booster rocket

Small engine for manoeuvring in space

9. Wheels are lowered ready to land

10. Landing on runway

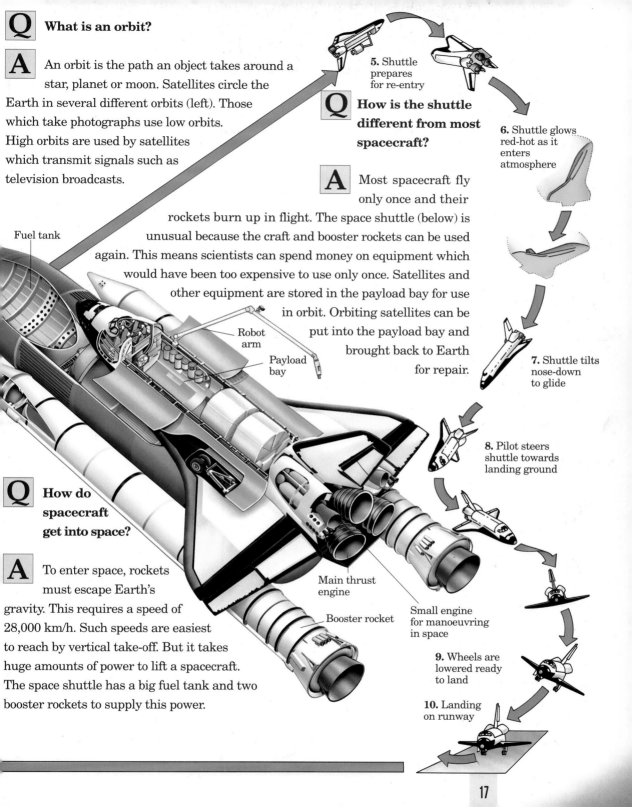

PLANET EARTH

Q What is inside the Earth?

A The thin outer layer of the Earth (below) is called the crust. Beneath this is the solid mantle that makes up most of the Earth. The mantle is a mixture of rocks and minerals. Right at the center of the Earth is the core of molten iron and nickel. The inner part of the core may be as hot as 6,500 °C.

Q How were the continents formed?

A Scientists believe that the continents (below) were formed from one giant landmass they call Pangaea. This broke in two, then split up into smaller landmasses. These drifted apart until they reached their present places. But they are still moving!

286–248 million years ago

213–144 million years ago

65–25 million years ago

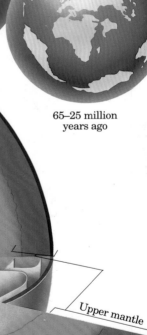

640 km

2,300 km

2,300 km

Lower mantle

Outer core

1,200 km

Inner core

Upper mantle

Crust

Q Why do we have seasons?

A The Earth takes one year to move around the Sun. But the Earth is tilted on its axis. This means that different parts of the Earth receive different amounts of sunlight, and so become warmer or colder as the Earth travels on its journey. When the North Pole is nearest to the Sun, the northern part of the Earth is warmest. Here it is summer. At the same time, the southern part is tilted away from the Sun, and is cooler. Here it is winter.

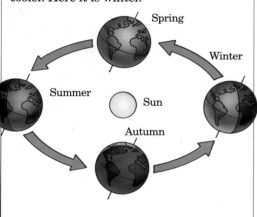

Spring

Winter

Summer

Sun

Autumn

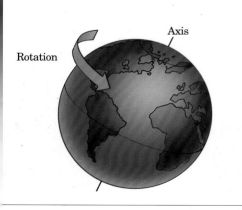

Rotation

Axis

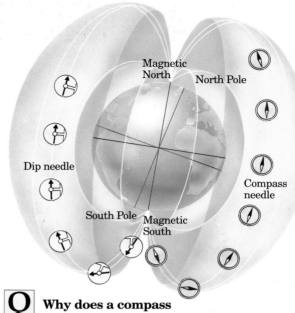

Magnetic North

North Pole

Dip needle

Compass needle

South Pole

Magnetic South

Q Why does a compass needle point north?

A The Earth is like a huge magnet with a force field that covers its whole surface (above). The poles of the magnet are near the North and South Poles. Magnetized objects – such as compass needles – are drawn to these poles. Therefore one end of a compass needle will always point north.

Q What were the ice ages?

A The ice ages (right) were periods in history when the Earth became extremely cold. The last ice age ended about 10,000 years ago. Near the poles, a lot of water froze into ice. This meant that there was less water in the sea and the sea level dropped, leaving large areas of land uncovered.

Earth during ice age

Earth today

NATURAL FORCES

Gas, ash and rock fragments

Layers of lava and ash

Crater left by previous eruption

Lava

Q Why do volcanoes erupt?

A Volcanoes erupt when hot molten rock from inside the Earth forces its way through cracks in the Earth's surface (above left). This rock, called lava, flows from the volcano and cools.

Q What is a seismograph?

A A seismograph measures earthquakes. When an earthquake occurs, its hanging arm shakes, and the pen marks the paper on the revolving drum.

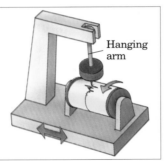

Hanging arm

Q What is a hurricane?

A A hurricane is a very strong whirling storm (right). The winds near the centre can reach 250 km/h. Hurricanes begin over warm tropical seas. The surface water heats up and evaporates to form clouds. This releases the heat and makes the clouds rise. Air is sucked in from the surrounding area, swirling the clouds into a spiral. At the very centre of the hurricane is a calm area called the eye. As hurricanes move, they push the sea into huge waves and may cause floods. When the hurricane reaches land, it slowly grows weaker. But the high winds can still cause great damage to buildings and trees.

Q How do we measure wind speed?

A The speed of the wind is measured on the Beaufort Scale. This goes from 0 (calm) to 12 (hurricane). The scale describes how things behave at different wind speeds (right). At 1, light air, smoke drifts slowly. At Force 6, large trees sway, and at Force 10, buildings may be damaged.

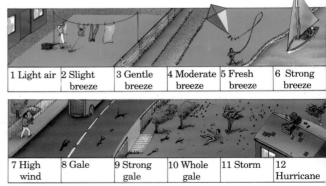

1 Light air	2 Slight breeze	3 Gentle breeze	4 Moderate breeze	5 Fresh breeze	6 Strong breeze
7 High wind	8 Gale	9 Strong gale	10 Whole gale	11 Storm	12 Hurricane

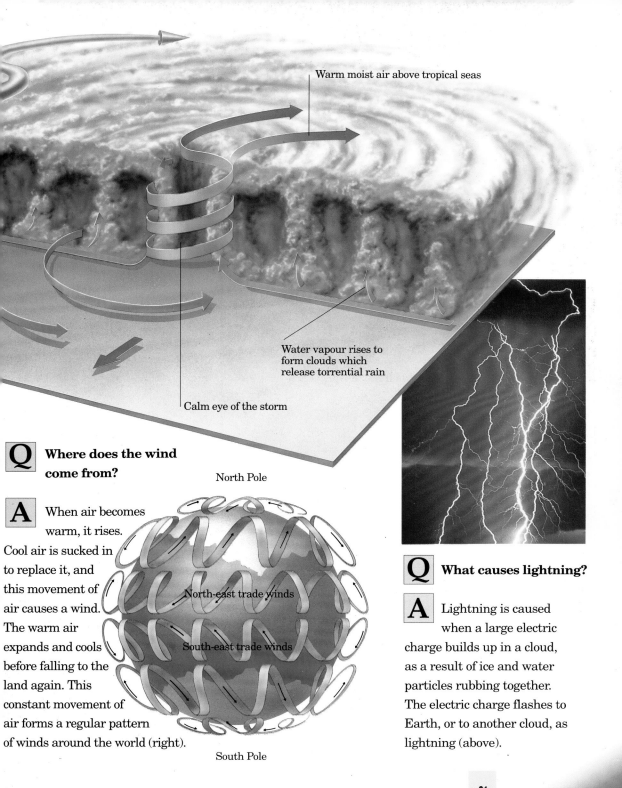

Warm moist air above tropical seas

Water vapour rises to form clouds which release torrential rain

Calm eye of the storm

Q Where does the wind come from?

North Pole

A When air becomes warm, it rises. Cool air is sucked in to replace it, and this movement of air causes a wind. The warm air expands and cools before falling to the land again. This constant movement of air forms a regular pattern of winds around the world (right).

North-east trade winds

South-east trade winds

South Pole

Q What causes lightning?

A Lightning is caused when a large electric charge builds up in a cloud, as a result of ice and water particles rubbing together. The electric charge flashes to Earth, or to another cloud, as lightning (above).

21

WATER

Q What lies under the oceans?

A The sea floor (below) has plains, valleys, mountains and even volcanoes. Near the shore is the shallow continental shelf. This slopes to the plain, about 4,000 metres below. On the plain are deep cracks called ocean trenches, and raised areas called ridges.

Continental Shelf   Ridge

Plain

Ocean trench

Q How much of the Earth is covered by oceans?

A The oceans cover 71 per cent of the Earth. The continents are actually huge islands in a continuous stretch of water (below). The water flows around the world in a pattern of warm and cold currents.

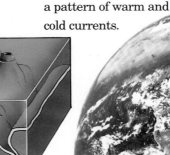

Q How does the sea change the coastline?

A The waves of the sea constantly pound the edge of the land (right). They change the shape of the coastline in two ways. First, the waves smash against the rocks and grind them into pebbles and sand. They hurl the pebbles at the cliffs, slowly wearing them away. But the sea also moves the sand and pebbles to other places. Beaches are formed and the coastline is built up where the sea drops them.

Waves wear away cliffs

Waves grind down pebbles to form sand

Q What is the water cycle?

A Water is always on the move (right), changing from liquid to vapour and back to liquid. The heat of the Sun evaporates water from the oceans, lakes and rivers. Plants also release moisture from their leaves. The moisture rises into the air and cools to form clouds. Winds blow the clouds towards the land. Here the clouds grow cooler, especially over high ground, and it starts to rain. The rain drains into rivers and lakes and then back into the sea.

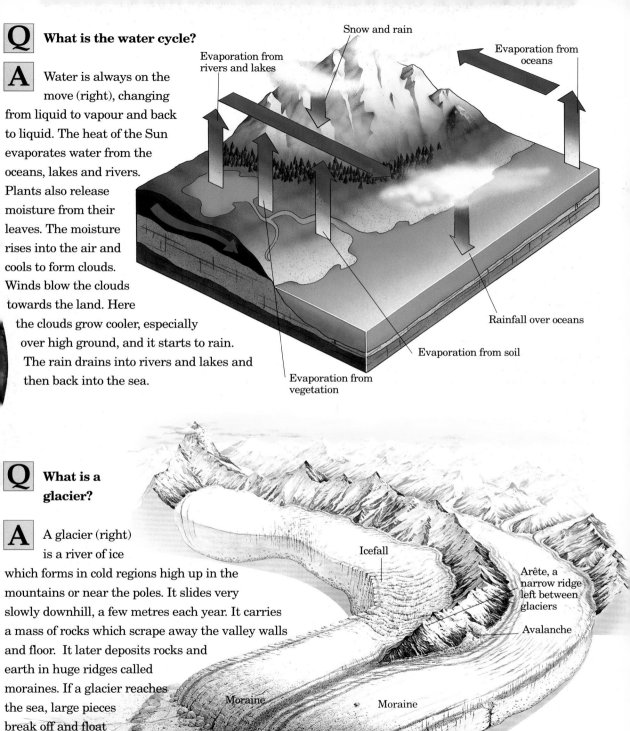

Snow and rain

Evaporation from rivers and lakes

Evaporation from oceans

Rainfall over oceans

Evaporation from soil

Evaporation from vegetation

Q What is a glacier?

A A glacier (right) is a river of ice which forms in cold regions high up in the mountains or near the poles. It slides very slowly downhill, a few metres each year. It carries a mass of rocks which scrape away the valley walls and floor. It later deposits rocks and earth in huge ridges called moraines. If a glacier reaches the sea, large pieces break off and float away as icebergs.

Icefall

Arête, a narrow ridge left between glaciers

Avalanche

Moraine

Moraine

LANDSCAPE

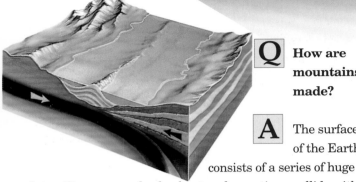

Q How are mountains made?

A The surface of the Earth consists of a series of huge plates. These move slowly about and sometimes collide with each other (above). When this happens, the edges of the plates are pushed up and the layers of rock crumple and fold. Over millions of years, the folds form chains of mountains.

Q How are caves formed?

A Many caves are found in limestone rock (below). They are formed when rainwater soaks down through cracks in the rock. The water dissolves the limestone, making the cracks bigger. Now streams can flow in underground. They wear away weak parts of the rock to make caves. Sometimes water drips into the caves. The dissolved limestone forms hanging spikes called stalactites. Pillars called stalagmites form on the floor below.

Q What is soil made from?

A Soil is a mixture of rock particles and humus, which is made from the tissues of dead plants and animals. The humus breaks down and releases minerals which help plants to grow. Below the soil is the rocky subsoil and beneath that the solid rock, known as bedrock.

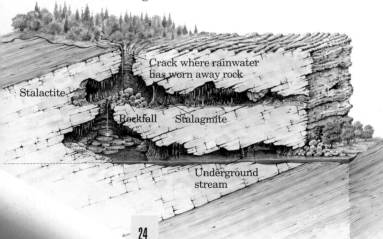

Crack where rainwater has worn away rock

Stalactite

Rockfall   Stalagmite

Underground stream

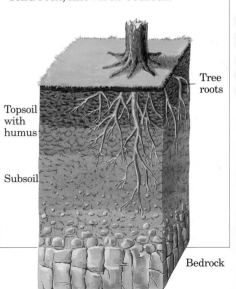

Tree roots

Topsoil with humus

Subsoil

Bedrock

Q How can a river alter the landscape?

A Rivers begin with water flowing downhill (left). Young mountain streams often originate in glaciers. The swiftly flowing water can carve away rock and produces deep V-shaped valleys. As it reaches the hills, it moves more slowly, producing broad valleys. When the river reaches flat plains, it may meander in wide curves. If a curve becomes cut off, it forms a lake. As a river reaches the sea, it deposits stones and sand to form a delta of low land along the coast.

Q What is an iceberg?

A An iceberg is a piece of ice from a glacier or polar ice sheet which breaks off at the coastline and then floats in the sea. Only one-eighth of an iceberg shows above the sea's surface. This is why they are dangerous to ships. Icebergs may drift for two years before melting.

Q How many different minerals are there?

A There are about 3,000 different kinds of minerals on Earth. Each is made from a different set of chemicals. Some minerals, like those forming rocks, may be quite common. Others, such as gold, silver and diamonds, are rare and precious. Minerals are used to make many things, from the lead inside pencils to the mercury inside thermometers.

Granite

Marble

Limestone

Slate

Pyrite

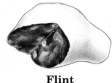

Flint

Sandstone

ROCKS & MINERALS

Tillite

Marble

Syenite

A There are three main types of rock – igneous, sedimentary and metamorphic (above). Igneous rock such as syenite is solidified lava. Sedimentary rock such as tillite is formed from compressed particles. Metamorphic rock such as marble is made from rock changed by heat or pressure.

Q How do we obtain rocks and minerals?

A Rocks and minerals are taken out of the ground by mining (below). If they are near the surface, they can be mined by scraping the earth away. This is open cast or strip mining. Deeper minerals are mined by shaft mining. Deep shafts are dug and miners tunnel out from the shafts to extract the minerals.

Q What are minerals?

A Minerals are non-living substances from which the Earth is formed. Some minerals combine together to form rocks. Olivine is a green mineral found in basalt. Quartz is the most common mineral on Earth. Galena contains lead.

Olivine

Galena

Quartz

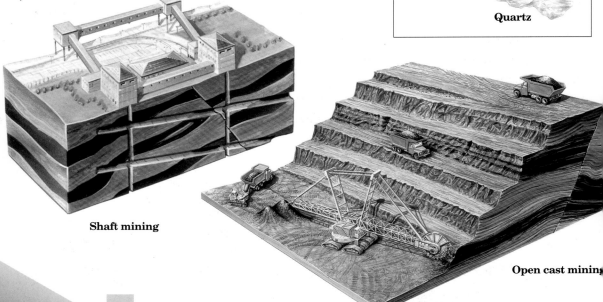

Shaft mining

Open cast mining

Q How did ancient people use stone?

A People have used stone for making things since prehistoric times. The first humans made axes and knives from flint. The Egyptians built stone pyramids to house the bodies of their kings. The Ancient Greeks built temples to their gods. The roofs were supported by massive stone columns. The Romans carved stone statues of their gods and leaders (right).

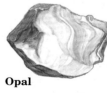
Pyramid building

Greek column

Roman statue

Q What are fossils?

Lepidodendron (a tree)

A Fossils are the remains of prehistoric animals and plants preserved in rock. When an animal or plant died, it sometimes sank into soil or mud. The animal or plant rotted away and its shape was replaced by minerals.

Ammonite (a shell)

Sea-lily

Q What are gems?

A Gems are rare and beautiful stones found in the Earth's crust. Most are crystals made of minerals. Opal and amethyst are two forms of silica. Sapphire is made of corundum. Diamond is made from a single element – carbon. Gems are cut to size, polished and made into jewellery with gold or silver (below).

Diamond

Diamond ring

Q How are rocks changed by heat?

A When hot, molten magma forces its way up through the Earth's crust (below), it changes the surrounding rocks. For example, limestone, which is soft and crumbly, becomes harder and changes into marble. The rising magma is called an igneous intrusion.

Opal

Sapphire

Amethyst

Igneous intrusion

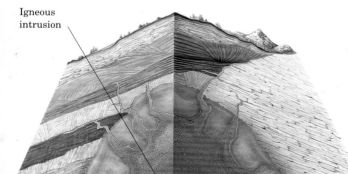

HABITATS

Q What is succession?

A Succession is the natural process by which habitats change, and one community of plants and animals is slowly replaced by another. The picture below shows an example of succession at work as a temperate lake silts up, and the dry land eventually becomes oak woodland.

Beaver's lodge

Q Can animals alter a habitat?

A Some animals can change their habitats. Beavers cut down trees with their strong teeth. Then they use the trees, together with mud and stones, to dam streams. Their homes, called lodges, are large piles of sticks built up from the bottom of the ponds they have created (above). Here, they raise their young, safely away from predators.

After 5 years

10 years

20 years

50 years

Lake

Plankton

Shark

Dolph

Bluefin tuna

Giant squid

Deep-sea jellyfish

Ska

Q What is a habitat?

A A habitat is a place where plants and animals live together as a community. Most creatures only live in one type of habitat, and cannot survive elsewhere. Look at the different habitats seen (right) in the picture of an ocean. Most life is found near the surface. A few species of fish and squid live in deeper water. The seabed is the realm of specially adapted marine creatures that cannot survive elsewhere in the ocean.

Angler fish

Q What are the world's main land habitats?

A The world's land habitats range from cold tundra and mountains, through hot deserts and grasslands, to the temperate woods and tropical rainforests, teeming with life. The ten major habitats are shown below. Each has its own type of climate, and plant and animal life.

Q How do wading birds avoid competing for food?

A These wading birds all have specially shaped beaks for catching different creatures on the seashore. So they do not compete for food although they live in the same habitat.

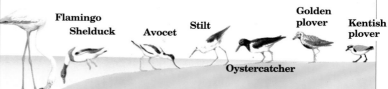

Flamingo
Shelduck   Avocet   Stilt
Golden plover
Kentish plover
Oystercatcher

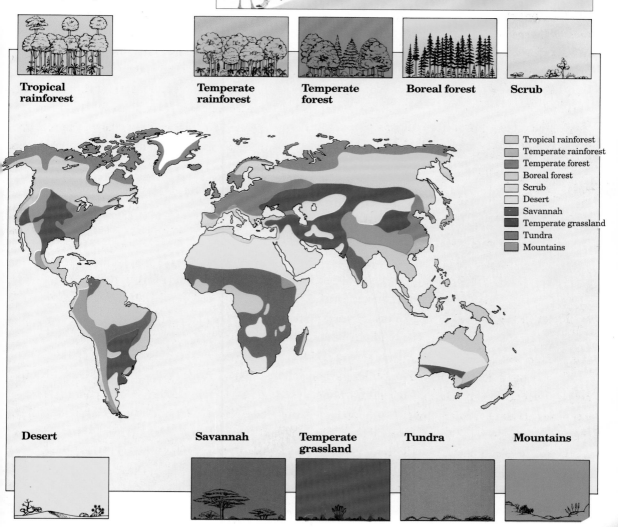

Tropical rainforest

Temperate rainforest

Temperate forest

Boreal forest

Scrub

Tropical rainforest
Temperate rainforest
Temperate forest
Boreal forest
Scrub
Desert
Savannah
Temperate grassland
Tundra
Mountains

Desert

Savannah

Temperate grassland

Tundra

Mountains

EVOLUTION

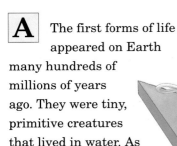

Q What is evolution?

A The first forms of life appeared on Earth many hundreds of millions of years ago. They were tiny, primitive creatures that lived in water. As millions of years went by, these creatures gradually changed and many different forms of life slowly appeared (above). This process is called evolution and it is still continuing today.

Q What does extinction mean?

A Extinction occurs when the last individual of a plant or animal species dies out. In the past, many creatures such as dinosaurs died out naturally – perhaps because of changes in the climate. In the last few centuries, animals such as the dodo (left) and the thylacine (below) have been hunted to extinction by people.

Q How do we know about the past?

A We find out about the past from fossils. If a prehistoric animal died in shallow, muddy water, its body might become covered with layers of silt which eventually formed solid rock. The soft parts decayed but the skeleton slowly absorbed minerals and hardened in the rock to become a fossil (left). Millions of years later, if the rock is worn away, we can find the fossils.

Q What is natural selection?

A Not all animals are as strong as others of the same species. This deer was not fast enough to escape a tiger attack and it will be killed. Other, fitter deer will evade capture and survive to breed. This process of survival of the fittest is called natural selection.

Q How did the horse evolve?

A The horse evolved from a rabbit-sized animal called *Hyracotherium* that lived 50 million years ago. Its descendants such as *Mesohippus* and *Merychippus* grew larger and became grazing animals. The number of toes in the foot dwindled from four to one, which improved its running speed and eventually the modern horse (below) evolved.

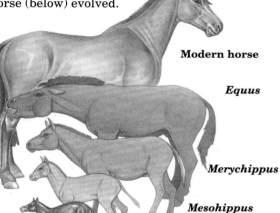

Modern horse

Equus

Merychippus

Mesohippus

Hyracotherium

Q What is adaptation?

A Animals and plants often develop traits that help them survive. Such traits are called adaptations. This tree-living tarsier is adapted with long legs for leaping, sucker-like clinging toes and large eyes for seeing at night.

Q When did our ancestors evolve?

A Our first true ancestor was the ape-like *Ramapithecus* (right). It lived about 8 million years ago, mainly in trees, but also foraged on the ground for food. Fossil bones have been found in Africa, Europe and India. *Australopithecus*, the next link in the chain, lived some 3 million years ago in East Africa.

PLANTS

Q How do plants spread their seeds?

A Plants have many ways of spreading their seeds (right). Some seeds grow inside fruits. These are eaten by animals and emerge in their dung. Some plants have seed cases which 'explode' or split open, throwing seeds in all directions. Some seeds, such as nuts and grains, are gathered by animals and stored in larders. Others have tiny hooks which cling to the coats of passing animals. Dandelion and maple seeds are so light that they are blown by the wind.

SEEDS CARRIED BY THE WIND

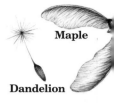

Maple

Dandelion

SEED INSIDE FRUITS EATEN BY ANIMALS

Fig

Blackberry

Plum

SEEDS CARRIED BY ANIMALS

Hazelnut

Wheat

Carrot

SEED CASES WHICH SPLIT OPEN

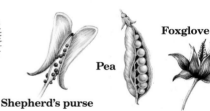

Shepherd's purse

Pea

Foxglove

Q What are the different parts of a flower ?

A The parts of a flower are attached to a base, called a receptacle. The outer green parts are called sepals. Inside these are the petals. Inside the petals are the stamens and the carpels: male and female parts which produce new seeds.

Receptacle

Petal

Sepal

Carpel (female)

Stamen (male)

Q Why are flowers brightly coloured?

A Flowers (below) have brightly coloured petals which attract bees and other insects. The insects feed on the sugary liquid called nectar inside the flower. Grains of pollen stick to these insects. When the insect visits another flower some of this pollen sticks to the new flower and pollinates it.

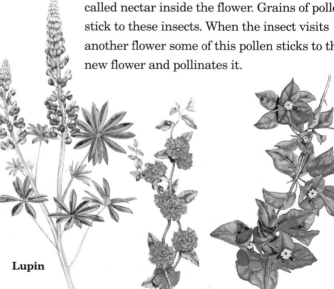

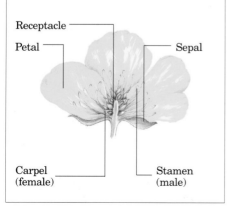

Lupin

Clarkia

Bougainvillea

Oxygen Sunlight

Carbon dioxide

Water

Water and minerals

Q How do plants grow?

A Plants need three things to make them grow – sun, air and water. The leaves absorb sunlight and a gas called carbon dioxide from the air. The roots draw up water and minerals from the soil. Cells in the leaves use the energy from the sunlight to change the water and carbon dioxide into sugar. This is the plant's food. In turn, the plant breathes out oxygen into the air. This process is called photosynthesis.

Cedar of Lebanon

Red fir cone   **Cedar cone**

Q How do plants survive in the desert?

A The soil of the desert is hard and dry. The air is very hot, and there is little rain. So desert plants have developed special ways of living in such a harsh place. Some, like the cactus (right), can store water in their fleshy leaves. The spikes help protect the plant from animals and also keep the leaves cool by casting tiny shadows.

Q What is an evergreen tree?

A Some trees have leaves which turn brown and fall off in the winter. Others lose only a few leaves at a time so there are always green leaves on the branches. These are called evergreen trees. One example is the Cedar of Lebanon (above). Some evergreens, such as holly and laurel, have broad leaves, but most have needle-shaped leaves. Because they are not thin and flat, these leaves do not lose moisture as quickly as broad leaves. Most of the needle-leaf trees also grow cones which carry their seeds. They are called coniferous trees and include pine, spruce, fir, cedar and larch.

ECOLOGY

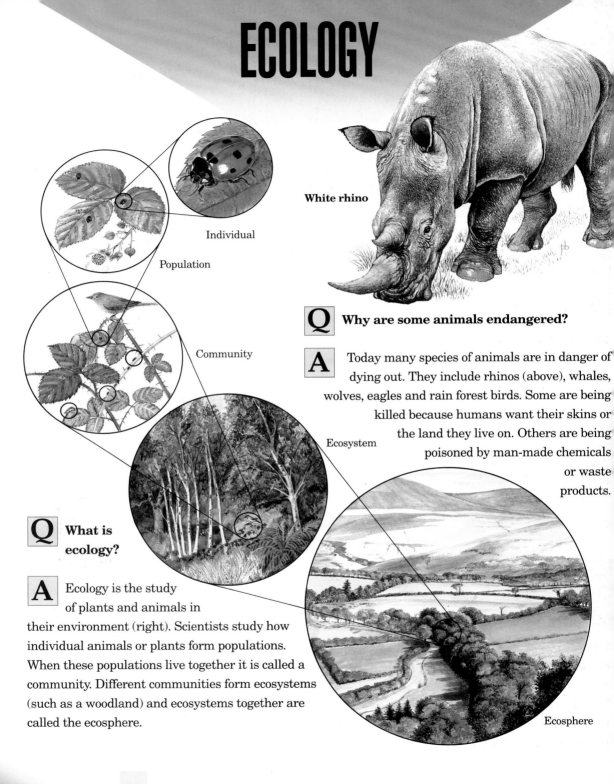

White rhino

Individual

Population

Community

Ecosystem

Ecosphere

Q Why are some animals endangered?

A Today many species of animals are in danger of dying out. They include rhinos (above), whales, wolves, eagles and rain forest birds. Some are being killed because humans want their skins or the land they live on. Others are being poisoned by man-made chemicals or waste products.

Q What is ecology?

A Ecology is the study of plants and animals in their environment (right). Scientists study how individual animals or plants form populations. When these populations live together it is called a community. Different communities form ecosystems (such as a woodland) and ecosystems together are called the ecosphere.

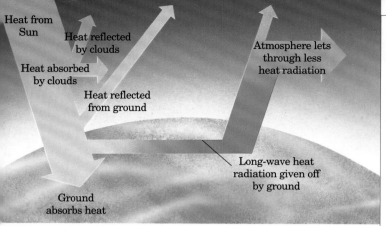

Heat from Sun

Heat reflected by clouds

Heat absorbed by clouds

Heat reflected from ground

Atmosphere lets through less heat radiation

Long-wave heat radiation given off by ground

Ground absorbs heat

Q What is the greenhouse effect?

A Heat comes to the Earth from the Sun. Most of it is then reflected back into space. But some gases trap the heat inside the Earth's atmosphere, which grows very hot like a greenhouse. This is what is known as the greenhouse effect (above).

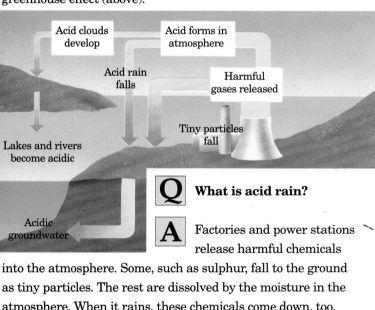

Acid clouds develop

Acid forms in atmosphere

Acid rain falls

Harmful gases released

Tiny particles fall

Lakes and rivers become acidic

Acidic groundwater

Q What is acid rain?

A Factories and power stations release harmful chemicals into the atmosphere. Some, such as sulphur, fall to the ground as tiny particles. The rest are dissolved by the moisture in the atmosphere. When it rains, these chemicals come down, too. This is called acid rain (above). It damages trees and other plants, and poisons the soil. Eventually acid rain drains into rivers and lakes, where it kills many fish.

Q Why are some insects called pests?

A Some insects harm people or crops. The Colorado beetle and the mint-leaf beetle damage food crops. The death-watch beetle destroys timber in buildings. The mosquito carries diseases.

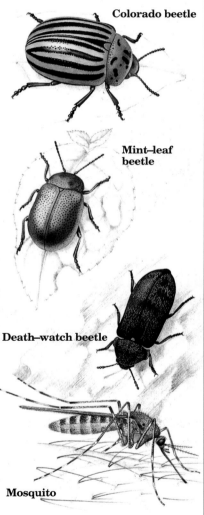

Colorado beetle

Mint–leaf beetle

Death–watch beetle

Mosquito

WORLD FACTS

Q Which is the world's largest country?

A Russia has an area of 17,075,400 square kilometres, making it the world's largest country. The second largest country is Canada, with an area of 9,976,140 square kilometres. Close behind it is China, with an area of 9,526,900 square kilometres.

Q Which is the biggest island in the world?

A Greenland is by far the world's biggest island, at 2,175,600 square kilometres.

Q Where is the biggest freshwater lake in the world?

A A lake is a large area of water surrounded by land. The biggest freshwater lake is Lake Superior in North America, which stretches for 82,350 square kilometres. Some of the largest lakes are actually seas, full of salt water. These include the Caspian Sea and the Aral Sea.

Q Which place has the least rain?

A The world receives an average of 86 centimetres of rain, snow and hail each year. But some places get little or no rain at all. The driest place in the world is Arica in Chile, which receives less than a tenth of one millimetre of rain a year. In parts of West Africa and South America, rain falls nearly every day.

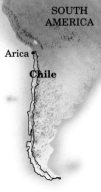

Greenland

Canada

NORTH AMERICA

Lake Superior

U.S.A.

ATLANTIC OCEAN

Sah

PACIFIC OCEAN

SOUTH AMERICA

Arica

Chile

ANTARCTIC OCEAN

Q Which is the world's smallest country?

 Q Which is the largest desert in the world?

A Vatican City is the world's smallest country. It covers only 44 hectares and lies inside another city – Rome, in Italy. Yet it is an independent state, with its own bank, railway station, and postage stamps. It is the centre of the Roman Catholic Church.

A A desert is a hot, dry region where there is low rainfall and little can grow. By far the biggest desert region is the Sahara in North Africa. This covers over nine million square kilometres. About one-seventh of the world's land area is desert.

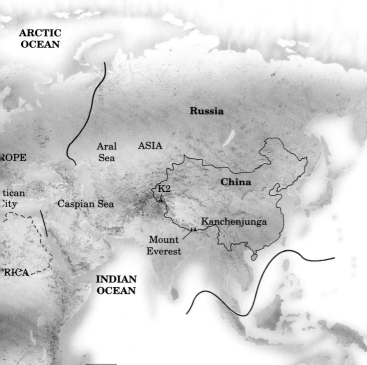

ARCTIC OCEAN

Russia

Aral Sea

ASIA

ROPE

China

K2

tican ity

Caspian Sea

Kanchenjunga

Mount Everest

RICA

INDIAN OCEAN

AUSTRALASIA

Q Where is the world's highest mountain?

A The world's highest mountain is Mount Everest. It lies in the Himalayas range in Central Asia and rises 8,848 metres above sea level. Some of the highest mountains in the world lie in this range. In the same range are K2 (8,611 metres) and Kanchenjunga (8,598 metres).

Q Where is the coldest place in the world?

A Antarctica is the coldest region in the world. It is the continent which surrounds the South Pole and is covered in a layer of ice about two kilometres thick. The temperature rarely rises above freezing point. In 1983, a temperature of -89.2 °C was recorded – the world's lowest ever.

ANTARCTICA

COUNTRIES & PEOPLE

Q Which continent has most countries?

A The continent with the most countries is Africa. There are 53 independent countries in Africa. The largest African country is Sudan. It has an area of 2,503,890 square kilometres. The African country with the most people is Nigeria, with a population of over 92 million.

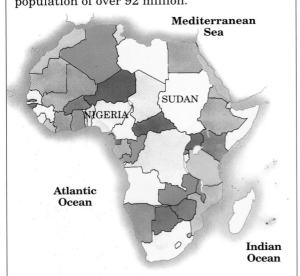

Mediterranean Sea

SUDAN

NIGERIA

Atlantic Ocean

Indian Ocean

Q Why do countries have flags?

A Every country has its own flag. Flags are used as a way of identifying the country, or anything belonging to it, to other nations. The flags above belong to countries that are members of the United Nations.

Q How many people are there in the world?

A More than 5,500 million people live on the Earth. By the end of the 20th century the population will have reached 6,500 million. Some places, such as deserts and polar regions, are largely unsuitable for people. Most people live where there is rich farmland or where cities can provide jobs and housing (below). The most populated country is China; it has over 1,000 million people.

Arctic Circle

Tropic of Cancer

Equator

Tropic of Capricorn

CHINA

Persons per sq km
over 500
201–500
101–200
51–100
11–50
1–10
less than 1

Antarctic Circle

Q How many races of people are there?

A Over many thousands of years, people in different parts of the world have developed variations in appearance and hair or skin colour. People of similar appearance and colour are said to belong to the same race. There are three main races: negroid, caucasoid and mongoloid (below). Their world distribution is shown on the map.

	Mongoloid
	Negroid
	Caucasoid

Q Why do people hold festivals?

A Festivals celebrate special days such as a time of year, like the Chinese New Year (below), or an important event such as the founding of a country, like Australia Day (right).

Q Why do people wear national costume?

A Modern dress is similar in many parts of the world, so many people remember their heritage by wearing a national costume on festival days. The costume usually has a long history. The Breton people of northwest France have a very distinctive costume (right).

PEOPLE AT WORK

Q How does a diver breathe under water?

A A diver uses scuba equipment to breathe underwater. Scuba stands for 'self-contained underwater breathing apparatus'. The diver (above) has metal tanks on his/her back that hold a mixture of oxygen and other gases so that the diver can breathe. The gases reach the diver's mouth through a hose.

Q What pre-flight checks must a pilot perform before take-off?

A The pilot has to check both inside and outside the plane before he takes off. In the cockpit (above), he checks that there is enough fuel for the flight and that all the engine and flight controls are all working properly.

Q What do vets do?

A Vets only spend part of their time in the surgery (left). There, they treat family pets, such as rabbits, dogs and cats. The rest of the time, vets travel to see bigger animals, especially on farms. They care for cows, pigs, sheep and other livestock and help to prevent the outbreak of animal diseases. Some vets inspect meat and eggs, or test milk and other animal products.

Q **How does a farmer prepare soil for crops?**

A First, the farmer ploughs the land (right). The sharp ploughshares dig into the soil and turn it over. To break up the lumps of soil, the farmer pulls a sort of rake called a harrow, either with discs or with curved spikes, over the field. He may also crush the lumps with a heavy roller. At this stage, fertilizers are spread on the field to make the crops grow quickly. Then the field is ready for sowing.

Ploughshare

Q **Which fish are caught by deep sea fishermen?**

A Most fish are caught by modern fishing boats. Nearly 80 million tonnes of fish are caught every year. The main fish caught near the seabed are cod, flounder, hake and pollock. These are often caught in funnel-shaped trawl nets. Fish enter through the net's wide mouth and collect at the narrow tail end. The fish must be preserved quickly or else they will spoil. Most deep sea fishermen pack their catch in ice (below), or deep freeze it, before sailing home.

Q **How much kit does a professional footballer use?**

A A league football club has 20 to 30 full-time players. Each player has at least five pairs of boots, including training shoes and special boots for use on hard ground. The team also uses nearly 1,000 pieces of clothing. These include match strip and tracksuits.

INDUSTRY

Q How is plastic made into shapes?

A In blow moulding (below), a piece of hot plastic tubing is placed in a mould. Air is blown into the tube, pushing it out into the shape of the mould.

Blow moulding

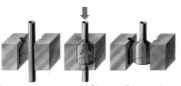

In vacuum moulding, plastic is placed over the mould and heated. Air is sucked out. This causes a vacuum which pulls the plastic down into the mould.

Vacuum moulding

Q How is coal mined?

A Most coal is mined by either the 'longwall' or 'room-and-pillar' method (right). In longwall mining a giant coal cutter runs down the coal face removing coal as it goes. In room-and-pillar mining the coal is removed from chambers, but pillars of coal are left behind to support the roof.

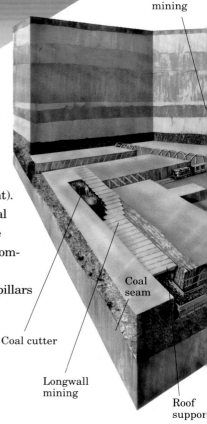

Coal seam

Coal cutter

Longwall mining

Roof support

Q What is paper made from?

A Most paper is made from wood (left). The wood is ground up or mashed into pulp using chemicals. The pulp is beaten so that the tiny wood fibres separate and soften. Then it passes on to a belt of wire mesh. The water drains through the mesh, and the pulp (now called the web) is squeezed first between heavy rollers and then between heated rollers. The dried and finished paper is wound on to reels.

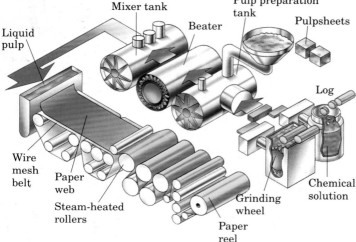

Mixer tank

Pulp preparation tank

Beater

Pulpsheets

Liquid pulp

Log

Wire mesh belt

Paper web

Steam-heated rollers

Grinding wheel

Chemical solution

Paper reel

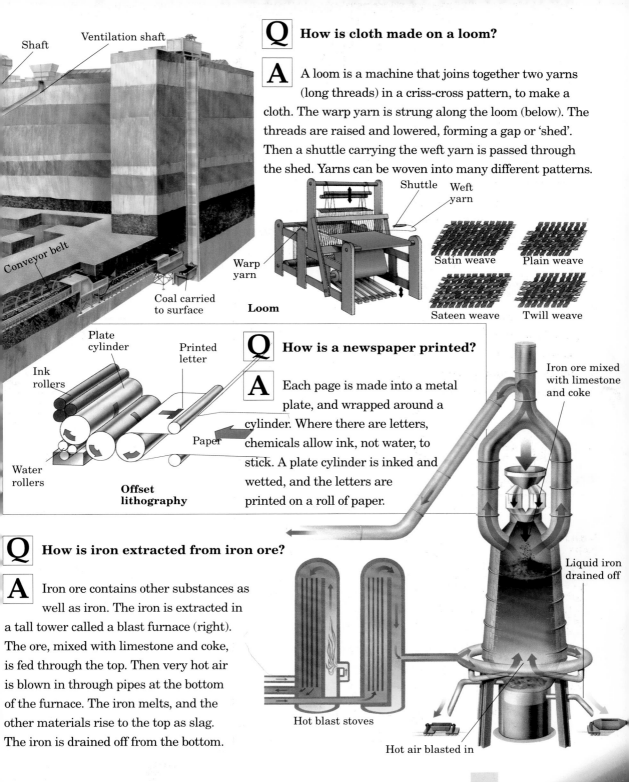

Shaft Ventilation shaft

Conveyor belt

Coal carried
to surface

Q How is cloth made on a loom?

A A loom is a machine that joins together two yarns (long threads) in a criss-cross pattern, to make a cloth. The warp yarn is strung along the loom (below). The threads are raised and lowered, forming a gap or 'shed'. Then a shuttle carrying the weft yarn is passed through the shed. Yarns can be woven into many different patterns.

Shuttle Weft
yarn

Warp
yarn

Loom

Satin weave   Plain weave

Sateen weave   Twill weave

Plate
cylinder   Printed
letter

Ink
rollers

Paper

Water
rollers

**Offset
lithography**

Q How is a newspaper printed?

A Each page is made into a metal plate, and wrapped around a cylinder. Where there are letters, chemicals allow ink, not water, to stick. A plate cylinder is inked and wetted, and the letters are printed on a roll of paper.

Iron ore mixed
with limestone
and coke

Liquid iron
drained off

Q How is iron extracted from iron ore?

A Iron ore contains other substances as well as iron. The iron is extracted in a tall tower called a blast furnace (right). The ore, mixed with limestone and coke, is fed through the top. Then very hot air is blown in through pipes at the bottom of the furnace. The iron melts, and the other materials rise to the top as slag. The iron is drained off from the bottom.

Hot blast stoves

Hot air blasted in

FARMING

Q How does a combine harvester work?

A A combine harvester (right) does nearly all the jobs in harvesting a cereal crop. At the front is the big pick-up reel. This pulls the crop into the cutter bar. The cut cereal is pushed by a rotating screw on to an elevator, which takes it to the threshing cylinder. This rotates very fast and separates the grain from the stalks. The grain is stored in a bin. When the bin is full, the grain is unloaded into a truck. The stalks are pushed out of the back of the harvester on to the ground.

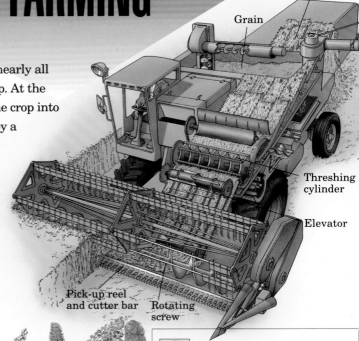

Stalks

Grain

Threshing cylinder

Elevator

Pick-up reel and cutter bar

Rotating screw

Rye

Oats

Barley

Maize

Sorghum

Wheat

Rice

Millet

Q Which plants are the most important source of food?

A Cereals are plants that produce grains (above). They are our most important source of food. The most common cereal is wheat. It is used to make bread or pasta and is the staple food of more than a third of the world's people. Rye, oats and barley are grown in northern Europe, mainly as animal food. Maize (corn) is a major crop in America and Africa, and rice is the staple grain of Asia. Sorghum and millet are also grown in Asia and Africa.

Q What is the cotton plant used for?

A The cotton plant grows in many of the warm parts of the world. The fibres which grow around the seeds are used to make cloth. The seeds are crushed to produce vegetable oil, or to make cattle food or fertilizers.

Q Why are there so many types of cattle?

A There are more than 200 breeds of cattle throughout the world. Many, such as this Friesian cow (right), are kept in herds to produce milk. Others, such as the Hereford, are raised for their meat. The hardy Zebu is best suited to the hottest parts of India and Africa.

Q Which products are made from milk?

A Milk has many uses. From the cow, it is pumped into the farm vat and then taken by tanker to the dairy. Here the milk is pasteurized (heated to kill the bacteria). If it is to be used for drinking, it is sealed into bottles or cartons. Milk can also be processed and turned into yoghurt, cheese, cream and butter.

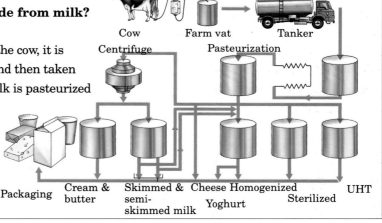

Cow   Farm vat   Tanker

Centrifuge   Pasteurization

Packaging   Cream &   Skimmed &   Cheese Homogenized   UHT
            butter   semi-   Sterilized
                        skimmed milk   Yoghurt

Q Which fruits grow in tropical areas?

A Tropical regions are hot all the year round. Here are some of the fruits which grow in these areas.
1. Pineapple, 2. Durian, 3. Carambola, 4. Mango, 5. Pawpaw, 6. Soursop, 7. Persimmon, 8. Mangosteen, 9. Pomegranate, 10. Litchi, 11. Akee, 12. Chirimoya, 13. Banana, 14. Guava, 15. Sapodilla, 16. Passion fruit, 17.Loquat, 18.Cape Gooseberry, 19.Rambutan.

Q Which countries have the most sheep?

A Australia is the biggest producer of sheep and wool in the world. In fact the country contains more sheep (about 156 million) than human beings. New Zealand is another major sheep producer, and contains about 20 sheep for every person! Many sheep are raised on the flat grasslands of South Africa, Argentina and Uruguay, as well as in China and India. Altogether, there are about 1,100 million sheep farmed throughout the world.

INDEX